First World War
and Army of Occupation
War Diary
France, Belgium and Germany

14 DIVISION
Divisional Troops
249 Machine Gun Company
16 July 1917 - 20 October 1917

WO95/1890/4

The Naval & Military Press Ltd
www.nmarchive.com
Published in association with The National Archives

Published by

The Naval & Military Press Ltd

Unit 10 Ridgewood Industrial Park,

Uckfield, East Sussex,

TN22 5QE England

Tel: +44 (0) 1825 749494

www.naval-military-press.com

www.nmarchive.com

This diary has been reprinted in facsimile from the original. Any imperfections are inevitably reproduced and the quality may fall short of modern type and cartographic standards.

Contents

Document type	Place/Title	Date From	Date To
Heading	WO95/1890/4		
Heading	14 Div Troops 249 Machine Gun Coy 1917 Jly-1917 Oct		
Heading	War Diary Of 249th Machine Gun Coy From 16 July 1917 To 31st July 1917 Volume 1		
War Diary	Grantham	16/07/1917	16/07/1917
War Diary	Havre	17/07/1917	20/07/1917
War Diary	Westoutre	21/07/1917	31/07/1917
Heading	War Diary Of 249th Machine Gun Company From 1st August 1917 To 31st August 1917 (Volume II)		
War Diary	Westoutre	01/08/1917	06/08/1917
War Diary	Chestre	07/08/1917	15/08/1917
War Diary	Wippenhoek	16/08/1917	17/08/1917
War Diary	Ouderdom	18/08/1917	18/08/1917
War Diary	Chateau Segard	19/08/1917	20/08/1917
War Diary	Trenches	21/08/1917	22/08/1917
War Diary	Chateau Segard	23/08/1917	25/08/1917
War Diary	Whippenhoek	26/08/1917	28/08/1917
War Diary	Thieushouk	29/08/1917	31/08/1917
Miscellaneous	From O.C. 249 Machine Gun Coy 14 (Light) Division Herewith War Diary For Period 1/9/17-30/9/17	30/11/1917	30/11/1917
Heading	War Diary Of 249 Machine Gun Company From 1/9/17 To 30/9/17 Volume 3		
War Diary	Thieushouk	01/09/1917	02/09/1917
War Diary	Mahutonga Camp	03/09/1917	30/09/1917
War Diary	Marseilles	04/10/1917	20/10/1917
War Diary	Neuve Eglise	01/10/1917	04/10/1917
War Diary	Marseilles	21/10/1917	28/10/1917
War Diary	Marseilles	04/10/1917	20/10/1917

14 DIV TROOPS

249 MACHINE GUN COY

1917 JLY — 1917 OCT

TO MESOPOTAMIA 18 IND DIV TROOPS

Confidential

Vol I

War Diary

of

249th Machine Gun Coy

from 16 July 1917 to 31st July 1917

Volume I.

Army Form C. 2118.

Instructions regarding War Diaries and Intelligence Summaries are contained in F. S. Regs., Part II. and the Staff Manual respectively. Title pages will be prepared in manuscript.

WAR DIARY
or
INTELLIGENCE SUMMARY.
(Erase heading not required.)

Place	Date	Hour	Summary of Events and Information	Remarks and references to Appendices
GRANTHAM	July 16/7/17	2.30a.	Entrained [illegible]	
HAVRE	17/7/17	10 a.m.	Disembarked [illegible] Proceeded to Rest Camp	
HAVRE	18/7/17		Lieut H.D.I.D BROWN admitted to hospital. Drew stores from Ordnance to complete equipment	
HAVRE	19/7/17 20/7/17	4 p.m.	In Camp Entrained	
WESTOUTRE	21/7/17	7 p.m.	Detrained at BAILLEUL and marched to Billets near WESTOUTRE. Company attached to 14th Division as Divisional Machine Gun Company	
"	22/7/17		In Billets. Training continued	
"	23rd			
"	24th			
"	25th			
"	26th			
"	27th		Three sub-sections (A, C & D) went on anti-aircraft duty at ammunition dumps near KEMMEL, DRANOUTRE and BAILEUL	
"	28th		Received orders that during forthcoming operations Division would be in Corps Reserve	
"	29th		In Billets. Training continued.	
"	30th			
"	31st			
"				

[illegible signature] Capt
O.C. 249. M.G. Company

(A7092). Wt. W12839/M1293. 750,000. 1/17. D. D. & L., Ltd. Forms/C.2118/14.

3

DI/14

Vol 2

Confidential.

War Diary

of

249th Machine Gun Company

from 1st August 1917 to 31st August 1917.

(Volume II)

Instructions regarding War Diaries and Intelligence Summaries are contained in F. S. Regs., Part II. and the Staff Manual respectively. Title pages will be prepared in manuscript.

WAR DIARY
or
INTELLIGENCE SUMMARY.
(Erase heading not required.)

Army Form C. 2118.

Place	Date	Hour	Summary of Events and Information	Remarks and references to Appendices
WESTOUTRE	1/8/17		Training Continued	
"	2/8/17		— do —	
"	3/8/17		"	
"	4/8/17		"	
"	5/8/17		" 3 subsections on Antiaircraft at TRENT DUMP, LOCRE, & DRANOUTRE relieved by 19th DIV.	
"	6/8/17		marched from WESTOUTRE to CAESTRE. Encamped at CAESTRE	
CAESTRE	7/8/17		Training Continued	
"	8/8/17		— do —	
"	9/8/17		"	
"	10/8/17		"	
"	11/8/17		"	
"	12/8/17		"	
"	13/8/17		"	
"	14/8/17		"	
"	15/8/17		marched from CAESTRE and camped in WIPPENHOEK area	
WIPPENHOEK	16/8/17		Training Continued	
"	17/8/17		marched to OUDERDOM (BILLETED.)	
OUDERDOM	18/8/17		marched to CHATEAU SEGARD Area Bivouacked	
CHATEAU SEGARD	19/8/17	10 a.m.	O.C. & Section Officers went up the line to reconnoitre positions for Barrage fire. Positions chosen along line from J19 a 6.8. to J19 C 5.8 (Ref sheet 28 ZILLEBEKE)	
"	19/8/17	7.45 pm	Working party composed of 4 Officers & 48 other ranks went up line and built gun emplacements on line chosen.	
CHATEAU SEGARD	20/8/17	8 a.m.	Working party returned to Bivouacs, having completed construction of 20 emplacements.	

(A7092). Wt. W12839/M1293. 750,000. 1/17. D. D. & L., Ltd. Forms/C.2118/14.

Instructions regarding War Diaries and Intelligence Summaries are contained in F. S. Regs., Part II. and the Staff Manual respectively. Title pages will be prepared in manuscript.

WAR DIARY
or
INTELLIGENCE SUMMARY.
(*Erase heading not required.*)

Army Form C. 2118.

Place	Date	Hour	Summary of Events and Information	Remarks and references to Appendices
Chateau Segard	20. 8. 17		At 2 pm small party took up 200 S.A.A. boxes by Light Railway to ZILLEBEKE. Carrying party of 3 Officers and 60 O.R started from camp 8. pm to take ammunition to gun positions, returning 4. am. Hostile shelling severe, casualties, 4 wounded, two of whom subsequently died of wounds	
TRENCHES.	21. 8. 17		At 7. pm. the Company (less 1 Sub-sec. of A and B Secⁿ) marched to gun positions arriving about 9 pm.	
"	22. 8. 17		Shortly before dawn small party went down to ZILLEBEKE to bring up remainder of ammunition. On return journey 3 men killed and 3 wounded by shell fire. All guns mounted and laid for Barrage by 6. am. Fire opened at 7.40. am and ceased at 10. am. Hostile shelling continued all day and increased in intensity at night fall. Company suffered irreparable loss in death of LIEUT T.W.M. WATSON. Casualties 1 officer, 4 O.R killed and 9 O.R wounded	
CHATEAU SEGARD.	23. 8. 17		At 6.20 pm. orders received to withdraw. Ration party suffered two casualties (2 wounded). Withdrawal completed 11-30. am.	
"	24. 8. 17		At dawn 3 Officers went up to the line with Divl M.G.O to reconnoitre new gun positions. Midday orders received to send Company to ECOLE, YPRES. Eight guns only available.	
"	25. 8. 17		At 4. pm orders received to concentrate at CHATEAU SEGARD	
WHIPPENHOEK.	26. 8. 17		10. pm. Company embussed and proceeded to billets near WHIPPENHOEK.	
"	27. 8. 17		Training continued	
"	28. 9 17			

(A7092). Wt. W12839/M1293. 750,000. 1/17. D. D. & L., Ltd. Forms/C.2118/14.

Army Form C. 2118.

Instructions regarding War Diaries and Intelligence Summaries are contained in F. S. Regs., Part II. and the Staff Manual respectively. Title pages will be prepared in manuscript.

WAR DIARY
or
INTELLIGENCE SUMMARY.

(*Erase heading not required.*)

Place	Date	Hour	Summary of Events and Information	Remarks and references to Appendices
THIEUSHOUK	29.8.17	10.am	Company marched with 42nd Bde to billets near THIEUSHOUK – distance 9 kilos. 14th Division transferred to 2nd Army (2nd Anzac Corps)	
"	30.8.17		Training continued	
"	31.8.17		" "	

G. T. Heyland

Capt

O.C. 249 Machine Gun Company

(A7092). Wt. W12839/M1293. 750,000. 1/17. D. D. & L., Ltd. Forms/C.2118/14.

From O.C. 249 Machine Gun Coy

To 14 (Light) Division

No. 249 MACHINE GUN COY.
No.
Date 30/9/17

Herewith War Diary for period 1/9/17 — 30/9/17

F Morhead
Capt
O.C.
No. 249 MACHINE GUN COY.

Army Form C. 2118.

Instructions regarding War Diaries and Intelligence Summaries are contained in F. S. Regs., Part II. and the Staff Manual respectively. Title pages will be prepared in manuscript.

WAR DIARY
or
INTELLIGENCE SUMMARY.

(Erase heading not required.)

Vol 3

Place	Date	Hour	Summary of Events and Information	Remarks and references to Appendices
			Confidential War Diary of 249 Machine Gun Company from 1/9/17 to 30/9/17 Volume 3.	

(A7092). Wt. W12839/M1293. 750,000. 1/17. D. D. & L., Ltd. Forms/C.2118/14.

Instructions regarding War Diaries and Intelligence Summaries are contained in F. S. Regs., Part II. and the Staff Manual respectively. Title pages will be prepared in manuscript.

WAR DIARY
or
~~INTELLIGENCE SUMMARY.~~
(*Erase heading not required.*)

Army Form C. 2118.

Place	Date	Hour	Summary of Events and Information	Remarks and references to Appendices
THIEUSHOUK	1.9.7		Training continued	
"	2. "		Marched to MAHUTONGA CAMP (RAVELSBERG AREA), distance about 16 kilos.	
MAHUTONGA CAMP	3 "	7.30. pm	Three Sub-sections proceeded to the line to occupy forward and barrage positions, in conjunction with 42nd Brigade.	
"	4. "		Training continued.	
"	5 "		" "	
"	6 "		" "	
"	7 "		Three Sub-Sections relieved those in the line. Relief complete 8.45. pm.	
"	8 "		Training continued.	
"	9 "		" " . Casualties – 1 man killed, 1 man wounded.	
"	10 "		" "	
"	11 "		Sub-Sections in the line relieved (Inter Company) Relief complete 8.15 pm	
"	12 "		Four guns proceeded to TRENT DUMP on anti-aircraft duty.	
"	13 "		In the line and on anti-aircraft duty	
"	14 "		" " " "	
"	15th		Inter-company relief of three sub-sections in the line. Relief complete 7.45 pm	
"	16 "		In the line and on anti-aircraft duty	
"	17 "		Six guns in the line fired a practice barrage from U.4.d. onto in conjunction with Artillery barrage.	
"	18 "		Six guns in the line fired practice barrage in conjunction with Artillery from U.4.d.	
"	19 "		In the line and on anti-aircraft duty.	

(A7092). Wt. W12839/M1293. 750,000. 1/17. D. D. & L., Ltd. Forms/C.2118/14.

W.H. / Capt.

Instructions regarding War Diaries and Intelligence Summaries are contained in F. S. Regs., Part II. and the Staff Manual respectively. Title pages will be prepared in manuscript.

WAR DIARY

or

~~INTELLIGENCE SUMMARY.~~

(Erase heading not required.)

Army Form C. 2118.

Cont'd

Place	Date	Hour	Summary of Events and Information	Remarks and references to Appendices
MAHUTONGA CAMP.	20.9.17	5.45am.	Six guns in the line fired a barrage in support of a raid by 41st Brigade; gun positions at ; target Number of rounds fired,	
"	21. "	2. pm	Four guns on anti-aircraft duty at TRENT DUMP relieved by Corps Cyclist Bn. Inter-company relief of guns in the line. One gun withdrawn. Relief complete 8. pm	
"	22. "		Training continued and in the line	
"	23. "		" " " " " "	
"	24. "		" " " " " "	
"	25. "		" " " " " "	
"	26. "		" " " " " "	
"	27. "		Inter-company relief of guns in the line. Orders received 7. pm to concentrate in camp midday 29th Sept. preparatory to entraining on 30th to proceed overseas.	
"	28. "		Five guns in the line relieved by 41st and 42nd M. G Coys.	
"	29. " } 30. " }		Company concentrated ~~at~~ in Camp in preparation of move.	

W. J. Heyland
Capt
O.C. 249. M. G. Coy

(A7092). Wt. W12839/M1293. 750,000. 1/17. D. D. & L., Ltd. Forms/C.2118/14.

WAR DIARY or ~~INTELLIGENCE SUMMARY.~~ 249 Machine Gun Coy

(Erase heading not required.)

Army Form C. 2118.

Place	Date	Hour	Summary of Events and Information
NEUVE EGLISE	Oct 1	6.30am	Marched to BAILEUL STATION and entrained about 9 pm with 207 M. G. Coy. Left at midnight destination MARSEILLES.
	2		En route
	3		
	4	[illegible]	Arrived MARSEILLES. Detrained and marched to FOURNIER CAMP. 207 239 238 M.G. Coys arrived in the course of the day.
[illegible]ES	5		In camp. The arrival of 24 more sections caused considerable congestion and made training very difficult. This was reduced to Physical Training
	6		and Route Marches. Drill clothing and topees were issued to all ranks.
	7		
	8		
	9		
	10		2 Officers and 100 O.R. detailed for fatigue duty at the docks. These
	11		went on board H.M.T.S. MINNETONKA and were quartered there.
	12		
	13		
	14		
	15		Remainder of Company went on board MINNETONKA with 336 and
	16		337 Bde R.F.A., 207 M.G. Coy and small parties of other units.
	17		Strength of Company on embarkation 10 Officers and 175 O.R.
	18		
	19		
	20	[illegible] pm	Sailed at 5 pm and anchored just outside
	21	[illegible] am	Sailed accompanied by two Japanese destroyers K and U.
	22		Owing to limited space, it was not possible to keep the kit and
	23		equipment of units separate. [illegible] in a certain number of
	24		losses. The reduced scale of rations was [illegible] felt by the [illegible]
	25		[illegible] found the [illegible] below decks very trying. [illegible] after PORT SAID
	26		it became necessary to clip all animals. One mule became seriously
	27		affected by the heat & had to be shot. The men were [illegible]
			[illegible] health remained good.

W. A. [illegible]
O.C. 249 M.G.C.

A5092. Wt. W12839/M1293 750,000. 1/17. D. D. & L., Ltd. Forms/C.2118/14.

www.ingramcontent.com/pod-product-compliance
Lightning Source LLC
Chambersburg PA
CBHW081512160426
43193CB00014B/2663
* 9 7 8 1 4 7 4 5 0 8 7 9 7 *